TRUE SOUND OF THE SACRED NAME OF GOD

TRUE SOUND OF THE SACRED NAME OF GOD

Brother Arnold Bowen

Xulon Press
2301 Lucien Way #415
Maitland, FL 32751
407.339.4217
www.xulonpress.com

© 2021 by Brother Arnold Bowen

All rights reserved solely by the author. The author guarantees all contents are original and do not infringe upon the legal rights of any other person or work. No part of this book may be reproduced in any form without the permission of the author.

Due to the changing nature of the Internet, if there are any web addresses, links, or URLs included in this manuscript, these may have been altered and may no longer be accessible. The views and opinions shared in this book belong solely to the author and do not necessarily reflect those of the publisher. The publisher therefore disclaims responsibility for the views or opinions expressed within the work.

Unless otherwise indicated, Scripture quotations taken from the King James Version (KJV) – *public domain*.

Paperback ISBN-13: 978-1-66282-403-6
Ebook ISBN-13: 978-1-66282-404-3

Table of Contents

Introduction.............................. vii

Chapter 1   The YH and Masoretic Vowels 1

Chapter 2   Transliteration 11

Chapter 3   Pure Truth from The Written
Word of God................... 17

Chapter 4   Hebrew has Vowels 19

Chapter 5   Stolen Identity 33

Chapter 6   Conclusive Evidence of the
Name Yuh 37

Chapter 7   SOUND of the Name............ 45

Chapter 8   The Vaw or the Wah SOUND...... 75

Chapter 9   What are our options concerning
the SOUND of the sacred
name of God? 79

Introduction

I've owned a septic tank company for over 40 years and have had the pleasure of meeting all kinds of neat people. I remember one time being out on a job and striking up a conversation with a fellow. I generally start by asking people if they know the name of God, and this makes for some really good discussions. I've found that most non-religious people will listen to me. It's the religious people I have trouble with.

When I asked this man if he knew the name of God Almighty, he got quiet and thought for a second; then he looked at me and said, "Doesn't it start with a Y?" I laughed a little bit, and he did too. I told him that we were talking about the name of the One who created everything we see: the dirt, trees, clouds, sky, moon, sun... and he could only say, "Doesn't it start with a Y?" He smiled, and then he listened to the information I had to share.

I want to share some of that information with you too. In this book I will conclusively prove what the SOUND of the name of God is. It's vital that you understand this fact right here at the beginning: a NAME is a SOUND. To prove this, all you have to do is speak your name. Go ahead, sound it out. In order to speak your name, you have to pronounce it; like with my name: Ar- nold. I've said it many times and others have as well. My name (and your name) is made up of particular letters, which when placed together form a sound. If someone wants to get my attention, they will SAY or SOUND OUT my name.

It's not different with the name of God, only much more important. Once we've found the SOUND of HIS name, we've actually found His name, because a name is a SOUND. Then, we can share this SOUND/NAME with others.

When we take this approach to finding the true name of God (the "Sound Approach") we can prove what God's name is once and for all, and everyone who calls on it can and will be saved (Joel 2:32). This is different from the approach used by wise and prudent scholars, who have for centuries tried to find out how to pronounce God's name by using uninspired vowels from the Masoretic (Hebrew) Text.

I often enjoy reading what the scholars and commentators have to say, but on this subject, I find it hard to rely on their conclusions. Most of them, after coming to a conclusion on how to say God's name, end up also saying that it's really not a big deal if we even use the Holy Name to start with. They are usually okay with substituting it for the words LORD and GOD, which are only common titles with no special significance. So I asked myself this question: "If wise and prudent scholars end up saying that we don't have to use God's Holy Name in our worship, praise, prayer, and teaching, should I believe that the actual SOUND of God's name is all that important to them?"

The fresh approach I am presenting here calls us to find the true SOUND of the Sacred Name. When we find it, we've found the genuine name of God Almighty, because (remember) a name is a **SOUND**.

I've never heard God's name make any other SOUND than this sound: YH. Go ahead and pronounce those two letters together, the very best you can. If you just did that you produced an involuntary "U" sound in between the Y and the H, sort of like a natural breathing sound. Say it again slowly and reverently. Listen to yourself as you pronounce these two letters.

This sound is especially noticed in a word that I'm sure you have heard before, whether you've ever been to church or not. My grandson even played this word for me in a popular song among the modern generation, a song sang by a man named Andy Grammar titled, "Good to Be Alive." Ever since he played this song for me, I like going back and listening to the part where the singer says, "I think I finally found my hallelu- Yuh!" Go and listen to the song. Andy Grammar speaks the sound of this word like everyone else across the earth.

This word is usually spelled "hallelujah," but the J is somewhat silent and pronounced as a Y, and the "ah" is pronounced as an "uh" sound. The pronunciation ends up being YUH, or just YH sounded out softly. This is similar to other English words that use the letter A. For example, say "what." Do you hear it? You pronounced the A with a soft U sound. More on this later.

This is also the sound found at the beginning and end of the names of prophets and holy men in Scripture. For example, Isaiah and Elijah. In both names the I and J are pronounced with the Y sound, and the "ah" is pronounced as a soft "uh." You may have never noticed this before, but you've likely spoken these names yourself and/or heard someone else speak these names.

I believe the SOUND of the name of God was embedded in this word of praise (hallelujah) and in the names of holy men (Isaiah, Elijah, etc.) long ago. This SOUND has been passed down from generation to generation and remains with us to this day. Churches all over the world speak the word hallelujah (ha-lle-lu-yuh) in their weekly meetings, yet many of them have no idea what the word means, or have ever thought that they are sounding out the name of God.

You might be thinking that all of this is just too simple, but isn't the answer to hard questions often hidden in simplicity? Sometimes a task that seems so hard ends up being accomplished in a simple way with the right tool. But if you have the wrong tool, you can't perform the task. I'm suggesting that we've been using the wrong tool. We've been looking at the Masoretic Text for too long, and it's led us down a rabbit hole in the wrong direction. We need to take off those glasses and put on a different set. We need to start fresh with this new approach I'm presenting.

This is something you don't even have to pray about. You just have to believe the SOUND of His Name that you've been hearing your whole life. Just like when you heard John 3:16, you didn't pray about it, you just believed that "God so loved the world that He gave his only begotten Son."

This is also not really something you have to study. I know that sounds a bit strange, but ponder on it. You hear with your own ears the SOUND of his name "YH" that is in the names of His prophets. You can also see this with your own eyes by simply bringing down the four letters of His name from Hebrew to English. Get rid of all the vowel points for a moment; they were added at a later date anyhow. The original Hebrew manuscripts only contained letters, no dots or dashes as vowel points. The letters of God's name are (from right to left):

These letters come down into English as YHWH, so you now see with your own eyes that there's no A or E vowel between the YH in the written Hebrew language. The A or E vowel is absolutely necessary for the name Jehovah or Yahweh. If it's not there in the original, it makes these names scripturally IMPOSSIBLE, a point I will develop in later chapters.

What we have to do here is simply believe, like a little child, and a little child has no problem pronouncing the YHWH as Yuh- Wuh, which is the correct transliteration of the Hebrew Yod-He- Waw-He. We must humble ourselves and become as little children to be saved (Matthew 18:3). If we don't add an A or E vowel between the YH, the YH will make a Yuh SOUND, as in Hallelu-YH, which is the name of God that went into all the earth (Exodus 9:16). It will also make the SOUND of the name of God that is in the holy prophets' names; names like Isa-Yuh, Jeremi-Yuh, Eli-Yuh, Yuh-hoo-dah, etc. This is no coincidence, because YH is his name, and is obviously SOUNDED Yuh, not Yah or Yeh.

Chapter 1

The YH and Masoretic Vowels

The following will show that the SOUND of the first two letters of the name of God, YH, is pronounced Yuh, as in Hallelu "Yuh", not Yah or Yeh. There is no A or E vowels between the YH in the original Hebrew, making the names Jehovah and Yahweh scripturally impossible!

If people would look up every scripture on name and see how important it is and how the Scripture teaches that his name is even above his word (Psalm 138:2) and in the last days whosoever calls on it shall be saved, Joel 2:32 and Acts 2:21, they would be more able to see why the devil does not want the true SOUND of his name out.

He put the SOUND of his name in the prophets' names, where it can never be lost. The SOUND of his name is still with us today, in the prophets' names, and the word Hallelu Yuh, and is not lost. There is none so deaf as he that refuses to hear, and none so blind as he that refuses to see.

How could we forget the SOUND of God's name that is in the name of Elijah (Eli Yuh), who shut up the heavens, who's name means my God is YH (Yuh), NOT Yah or Yeh.

The SOUND of God's name that is in Elijah's name, was already establish "before" the Masoretic vowels, and therefore the SOUND of his name was not affected by them, and that's why we say Eli Yuh the prophet.

The same with all biblical names with the name of God in their names, the SOUND of his name is there and will always be.

We have a Scriptural right to say his name is YH, pronounced Yuh, but they do not have a Scriptural right to say it's anything else, because there's no "a" or "e" vowels between the YH, anywhere in the original Hebrew, for the names Jehovah and Yahweh!

We will show how the Masoretic vowels were added later, but not by the Masoretes. The Masoretes added vowels from Adonai and Elohim, AROUND the sacred name to remind the reader not to read the sacred name Yuh, but to say a substitute names like Adonai or Elohim, but not the name YH or YHWH, and someone later, not understanding that, added the uninspired Masoretic vowels to the sacred name, which the Masoretes would never do, as some suggest. As a matter of fact, they had their chance to add it over 7,049 times and never did.

This article shows there is a way to know 100% sure what the "SOUND" of the name of God is, no guessing, speculating, assuming, conjecture etc, which has been going on for many years now.

It's so easy, we can easily find out what his name SOUNDS like, and simply repeat it. His name is in all of the prophets' names and their names are handed down to us, just like his name in Hallelu Yuh.

We actually know what his name SOUNDS like, because of the fact that he put it in his prophets' names, and it is handed down to us, to never be lost or forgotten.

It is clearly written in other names too, like Yhoshua, pronounced Yuh shua or Yhoshua

H3091 (Strong) says,
יְהוֹשֻׁעַ יְהוֹשׁוּעַ
yᵉhôshûaʿ yᵉhôshûaʿ
yeh-ho-shoo'-ah, yeh-ho-shoo'-ah

From H3068 and H3467; *Jehovah-saved*; *Jehoshua* (that is, Joshua), the Jewish leader:–Jehoshua, Jehoshuah, Joshua. Compare H1954, H3442.

Notice in the original Hebrew, the E vowel is not a part of the name, there's no E between the YH in Hebrew!
יְהוֹשׁוּעַ

Once we hear the SOUND of the name of God, we then know what it is, because a name is a SOUND!

Whatever the SOUND of his name is, that's his name, and nothing else matters. There's nothing else to even consider, no other options.

To debate all that other stuff that is contrary to the SOUND of his name in the prophets' names is immaterial and irrelevant, the debate is over, once we believe what our ears have been hearing all our lives since birth.

We can read and research all that different scholars have written on the name, most of which cannot be understood and has not been proven, and they don't even agree among themselves, or we can simply believe the SOUND of his name that we hear every day, that even a country boy like me can understand and be saved.

All of us can understand the SOUND of a name, so don't let them talk you out of it, pretending that they know something you don't.

The SOUND of his name is in the prophets' names and that SOUND is the same today, yesterday, and forever, and is a memorial to all generations, Exodus 3:15. The names Yahweh and Jehovah has never been memorialized and handed down to us like his name Yuh, that went into all the earth in Hallelu Yuh has.

It may surprise you to know that everyone reading this article already knows the true name of God, they just don't realize it yet, partly because of all the confusion brought on by the wise and prudent scholars, which something is hid from, Luke 10:21, and Matthew 21:25.

Again, a name is a SOUND and different names have different SOUNDS to distinguish one from another.

The name YH or YHWH means the SELF EXISTING one, or the one who causes everything that "is", "to be", he just says "be", and it is.

None can claim they "self" existed, and therefore he alone can claim the name YHWH, which distinguishes him from all other so-called Gods etc.

Therefore, if we SOUND or add an "a" or "e" vowel between the YH, of his name, we are actually creating a different name and different SOUND, making void the original name of God, bringing it to naught, and giving glory for what God has done, and who he is, to a totally different name, a name that is not the name of the one who alone self exists! The SOUND of no other name under heaven other than Yuh, represents The Self Existing One, The Creator of heaven and earth.

Isaiah 42:8 says, "I am the LORD: that is my name: and my glory will I not give to another, neither my praise to graven images."

We are in trouble if we give glory and credit to another name, instead of the name that all glory and honor belongs to.

Let me get this out-of-the-way. Some are saying that Abraham, Isaac, and Jacob did not know the name YHWH, which is also a mistake.

Abraham Issac, and Jacob knew God's name YHWH

Genesis 15:2 says,
2 "And "Abram" said, Lord "GOD" (YHWH), what wilt thou give me, seeing I go childless, and the steward of my house *is* this Eliezer of Damascus?"

Genesis 15:7
7 "And he said unto him, I *am* the "LORD" that brought thee out of Ur of the Chaldees, to give thee this land to inherit it."

And "Abraham" called the name of that place *Jehovah*jireh: as it is said to this day, In the mount of the "LORD" it shall be seen. Genesis 22:14

Abrham knew his friends name, and so did Isaac and Jacob!

Gen 27:20 "And "Isaac" said unto his son, How *is it* that thou hast found *it* so quickly, my son? And he said, Because the "LORD "thy" God" brought *it* to me."

Gen 28:16 "And "Jacob" awaked out of his sleep, and "he said", Surely the "LORD" is in this place."

How do we then harmonize this next verse?

"And I appeared unto Abraham, unto Isaac, and unto Jacob, by the name of God Almighty, but by my name *JEHOVAH* "was" I not known to them. Exodus 6:3

First of all it does not say "I "was not" known to them, but "was" I not known to them???

The word "was" I not known" is asking a question, and therefore a question mark belongs after the question!

It obviously should read, "And I appeared unto Abraham, unto Isaac, and unto Jacob, by the name of God Almighty, but by my name *JEHOVAH (YHWH)* "was" I not known to them? Sorta a rhetorical question.

Chapter 2

Transliteration

There's a difference between "Translate" and "Trans-literate".

Translate is to tell the "meaning" of a word in another language, while transliterate is to tell the "SOUND" of names of people and cities etc.

Names of people and Cities do not change from language to language, but stays the same in every language, same as his name in Hallelu Yuh, said the same in every language and dialect on earth.

It is especially important to know these fundamental FACTS about Transliteration.

The Transliterated "SOUND" of our English letters, YHWH, is equivalent to the "SOUND" of the Hebrew letters Yod He Waw He, and when the Yod He Waw He is pronounced by a Hebrew speaking child, the SOUND is Yuh Wuh, and when the YHWH is pronounced by an English-speaking child, the SOUND is also Yuh Wuh! That's what Transliteration is.

The Hebrew letter Yod has the same exact SOUND as our English letter Y, and the Hebrew letter HE has the same SOUND as our English letter H, and the Hebrew letter Wah, has the same SOUND as our English W.

If Moses spoke English and heard the SOUND of God's name, he would have written YHWH, and pronounced it Yuh Wuh, exactly like we do today. He captured the SOUND with letters, and published it, Deuteronomy 32:3.

It's the same with the Transliterated name of the city Hong Kong, or the "name" of anything for that matter.

Take Chinese children that are learning to read and have them pronounce the Chinese letters for Hong Kong, and they will say Hong Kong, and have English speaking children pronounce the equivalent English letters for Hong Kong, and they will say the same SOUND, Hong Kong.

When the "SOUND" of a single letter from one alphabet is brought over to another language and finding a letter in that language that makes the same SOUND, that is transliteration, and when you do several alphabet letters of a name, the name will "SOUND" the same in BOTH languages!

Once we find out what the SOUND of the transliterated name of God is, we simply pronounce it as written, we don't try to figure out what "else" to add to the already Transliterated "SOUND", that's already taken care of in the transliteration process!!!!!!

Once we transliterate the sound of the name of a city like Hong Kong, Bethlehem, Nazareth, or any name, into English, we then simply say it, we don't try to figure what else to add to the already transliterated SOUND, and this is especially true with the SOUND of the name YHWH, pronounced Yuh wuh!!!

Again, Transliteration is taking the SOUND of one letter of an alphabet and bringing it over into another language by finding a letter of that alphabet that makes the same SOUND of the letter that its being transliterated from, its SOUND for SOUND.

The Hebrew letters Yod He Waw He, makes the same exact SOUND as our English letters YHWH, which is pronounced Yuh Wuh in both languages. This fact alone should settle what the SOUND of his name is. Other languages have alphabet letters that can make the exact same SOUND as the Yod He Waw He.

That's why, names of people and cities like Hong Kong, China or New York and YHWH, is pronounced the same everywhere in the world, same as Hallelu Yuh, and also the prophets' names with the same YUH SOUND in their names.

The SOUND of YHWH is NOT Jehovah or Yahweh, its Yuh Wuh! Are you listening?

Whatever SOUND that the Hebrew alphabet letters, Yod He Waw He makes in the Hebrew alphabet, the SOUND of these letters is transliterated into other languages by finding which letters of their alphabet, makes the same SOUND as the Hebrew Yod He

Waw He letters. In English, it is our YHWH that makes the same SOUND, and then all we have to do is Pronounce it, but someone chose to add uninspired vowels to the name even after the SOUND is Transliterated, changing the original SOUND, and a name is a SOUND, and when we change the original SOUND, we change the original name, and gave glory and praise to a totally different name that does not represent our Great God.

Once Transliterated it reads Yuh Wuh, and this is what SOUND that Moses heard God say his name is in Exodus 3:15, and that SOUND is his name and a memorial to ALL generations. The Devil don't want people to know it.

We get a slight U vowel SOUND, which is an involuntary SOUND, that comes naturally when pronouncing the consonants or vowels of YH-WH.

In both the Old and New Testament, Bethlehem is called Bethlehem, and is Bethlehem in every language and dialect, on earth, Hebrew, Greek, Aramaic, English, Russian, Chinese, German, and every language in the world, because the SOUND of names are

Transliterated SOUND for SOUND from one language to another, just like the SOUND of the name YHWH. That's how his name in Hallelu Yuh is SOUNDED the same in every language in the world. His name is Yuh. You may write it Yah or iah, but it is still SOUNDED Yuh, as in Isaiah/IsaYuh, Jeremiah/JeremiYuh, etc!

Once the Hebrew letters, that Moses used to write down the SOUND of the name of God that he heard, Exodus 3:15, has been "Transliterated", not "Translated", into another alphabet, it is then ready to be pronounced, and we will get the same SOUND of the sacred name that Moses heard and wrote down, in our own language!

Even if they try to get around this fundamental fact about Transliteration, they still have the fact that his name is SOUNDED Yuh in all his prophets' names, and there's no way to change or get around that SOUND, which is still with us today, same as Hallelu Yuh.

Chapter 3

Pure Truth from The Written Word of God

When we accept the word, as written, it "does not" have an "a" or "e" vowels between the YH of his name, which is needed to make the SOUND of Yah and Yeh, and THIS ALONE is positive proof that his name can't be Yahweh or Jehovah!

You cannot have the name Yahweh or Jehovah without adding an "a" or "e" between the YH, and if none exists in the original written Hebrew, both names are not the name of the Almighty self-existing one! That is an absolute. These names are actually founded on the added uninspired Masoretes vowels. Is that what we want???

Where did the added "a" and "e" vowels between the YH come from, if they were not originally in the written Hebrew text???

They were obviously added at a later date by someone who mistakenly thought the Masoretic vowels were to show the pronunciation of the name but were actually added under the name to remind the reader not to read the name YHWH (Yuh Wuh), but to say Adonai (master) or Elohim (God) instead, because they followed the tradition not to say the sacred name because it is too Holy. Look up the name Jehovah, for more information.

The unmolested YH, makes the Yuh SOUND, as in Hallelujah, pronounced Hallelu Yuh, and is also pronounced the same in in every language and dialect on earth. This is no coincidence, it is caused by "Transliteration", of his name Yuh.

Chapter 4

Hebrew has Vowels

Now for those who have been told that the Hebrew has no vowels, is not true, but even if it were true, it would still not change the SOUND of his name because we get involuntary vowels SOUND that comes naturally when trying to sound the consonants, just like the slight U SOUND when pronouncing the YH-(Yuh).

Much of the error of the scholars is founded on the assumption that the Hebrew does not have vowels, which is just NOT TRUE and if we can prove it is not true, their whole argument is worthless, because that's their excuse for adding extra vowels to the already Transliterated 4 letter name, called the Tetragrammaton!

The Hebrew Yod He Waw He serves as vowels and consonants; they are called Semivowels. This you can easily verify for yourself.

The encyclopedia says,

Matres lectionis (from Latin "mothers of reading", singular form: mater lectionis, from Hebrew: אֵם קְרִיאָה 'em kəri'a) are consonants that are used to indicate a vowel, primarily in the writing down of Semitic languages such as Arabic, Hebrew and Syriac. The letters that do this in Hebrew are "aleph א, he ה, waw ו and yod י," and in Arabic, the matres lectionis (though they are much less often referred to thus) are 'alif ا, wāw و and yā' ي. "The 'yod and waw in particular are more often vowels than they are consonants."

The original value of the matres lectionis corresponds closely to what is called in modern linguistics glides or "semivowels." See https://en.m.wikipedia.org/wiki/Mater_lectionis

They used to teach in school that the vowels are AEIOU, sometimes Y and W too. Yes, even in English the Y and W can be vowels.

If the Hebrew has vowels, "and it does", their whole argument falls, because that is their excuse for adding either the A or E vowel to the sacred name to make it say Yahweh or Jehovah!

If what they are saying the SOUND of his name MIGHT be, does not match the SOUND that we are HEARING, what should We do?

What should we believe, the SOUND that our ears are hearing, or the words their mouths are saying?

Some men love flattering titles, they want to be called Doctor etc, but doctors lie for different reasons, look at dr. Fauci.

Job said, in Job 32:21-22 KJV
[21] "Let me not, I pray you, accept any man's person, neither let me give "flattering titles" unto man. [22] For I know not to give "flattering titles"; in so doing my maker would soon take me away."

The Dead Sea Scrolls and other ancient writings never had these added vowels and didn't need them to say what they had to say.

Josephus, a Hebrew scholar who actually saw the name of God on the head gear of the high priest, "says" it consists of "four vowels". The War of the Jews, Book 5. 5. 7.

Again, it does NOT matter whether the YHWH consists of 4 vowels, consonants, or semivowels, the SOUND of the name is what it is, and when it is transliterated, it has the Yuh SOUND, and it is also the Yuh SOUND that it makes in the Prophets names, and the word Hallelu Yuh, it does not change the SOUND one bit, because even when we try sounding consonants, we get an involuntary vowel sound!

As mentioned above, the Yod He and Wah are used as vowels and consonants, and the Yod and Wah is "more often used as vowels than consonants", and if we add another A or E vowel between the YH, we have "Two vowels together" and we are taught in school that "When two vowels go walking, the first one does the TALKING." The first one is the Yod vowel, which makes the Yuh SOUND.

There are many cases in which two vowels "go walking," including ai, au, ea, ee, ei, ie, oa, eo, oi, oo, ou, and ui. And when a pair of vowels appears in a word, it is the first vowel that "does that talking," as represented in words like green, sea, hair, coat, clean, rain, peach, and onion etc. Side note: Notice the "i" in onion is still pronounced with the Y sound (onYuon), and it is doing the talking.

Side Note: If Josephus saw 4 vowels, then the Y and W would do the talking and say Yuh Wuh, according to the linguistic walking talking rule.

We know that whether this linguistic rule is always true or not, it is true in this case, BECAUSE of the Yuh SOUND that the two walking vowels in iah (YAH) makes in the Prophets names ending in iah, like Isaiah, Jeremiah, Nehemiah, Zechariah, Obadiah, etc which is SOUNDED Yuh, and the A is silent, because Y is the first vowel, followed by the A vowel and therefore does the talking and is pronounced Yuh, proving they were following the rule!

If this rule was not being followed, the name of God, "iah", at the end of the prophets names, WOULD NOT be pronounced Yuh, but we know and hear that it is, and we can believe our own ears!

His name, that is in the Prophets names, makes the Yuh SOUND, not a Yah sound!

All the prophets' names ending in the Father's name, spelt iah or jah, is ALWAYS pronounced with the Yuh sound, and the A is silent BECAUSE the Y is talking, which is pronounced Yuh, therefore they obviously followed the walking together rule.

The Yuh SOUND is doing the TALKING, but are people listening?

Here are just a few of the many names with the Father's name, Yuh, in their names, ending in iah and jah, understanding the i and j is a Y in Hebrew which could be a Yah sound UNLESS the Y is used as a vowel, and then it makes the Yuh SOUND because we have TWO vowels walking together, and the first one does the TALKING, which is pronounced Yuh, and the Yuh SOUND of his name in the prophets names positively proves the Y is a vowel, or it would make the Yah sound in the prophets names, but it does NOT, it makes the Yuh SOUND. Please listen.

The names ending in iah and jah, but still makes the Yuh SOUND, because the Y is a vowel, followed by another vowel, and the Y/Yuh SOUND is doing the talking.

Isa"iah", which means Yuh has saved, Jerem"iah", which means Yuh will rise, Nehem "iah", which means consolation of Yuh, Obadiah, which means serving Yuh, Eli "jah", which means, my God is Yuh, Hallelu "jah", which means praise Yuh, etc, and there is many more, and not even one is pronounced Yah or Yey, but ALWAYS Yuh!

There are too many biblical names to mention, which has the Father's name in their names, names ending in "iah", but here is a website that has all of them listed, and their meanings, which meaning is Yuh this or Yuh that. https://www.behindthename.com/names/pattern/*iah

If all the biblical names of the prophets names, having the Father's name in theirs, the "iah" making the Yuh SOUND, which is actually "Yah" instead of "iah", but is pronounced or SOUNDED Yuh, then Psalm 68:4 actually says his name is Yah also, and would be pronounced or SOUNDED Yuh, the same as the "iah", which is Yuh, because the Y vowel is walking with an A vowel, just like in "iah", and the first vowel does the talking, just like in "iah", and therefore Psalm 68:4 is pronounced Yuh also, not Yah.

Psa 68:4 Sing unto "God", sing praises to his "name": "**extol**" him that rideth upon the heavens by his "name JAH", and rejoice before him."

Exo 15:2 says, "The LORD *is* my strength and song, and he is become my salvation: he *is* my God, and I will prepare him an habitation; my father's God, and I will exalt him."

His name in Psalm 68:4 is pronounced Yuh, just like the iah at the end of the prophet's names, the added A vowel is silent just like it is in the iah.

The same is true with the vowels WE together, the Hebrew Waw (W) does the talking and is pronounced Wuh, not Weh as in YahWeh, or YahWay, but Yuh, as in Hallelu Yuh.

Therefore, even if Yahweh is written one way, it is still pronounced Yuh Wuh, because in Hebrew, the Y and W are more often vowels than consonants, and even in the English language, the Y and W can be used as vowels, and the second added A vowel is silent, because of the linguistic two vowels together rule.

If his name is not Yuh, then there's no way to conclusively prove what it is, and we cannot trust anyone who adds an uninspired A or E vowel into the sacred Name YH and the YHWH, when it's not in scripture. They are actually adding to the word of God, when they do this.

If all the short forms of the name YH, like Psalm 68:4 has an A vowel added between the YH, and the long form YHWH has an E vowel between the YH, which is it???

Does it make sense that the SOUND of the YH in the short form be Yah, and the SOUND of the YH in the long form be Yeh?

That is confusion, and God is not the author of confusion.

If they would just leave the name YH alone, it will make the SOUND Yuh, as in Hallelu Yuh, the name that went into all the Earth and the Yuh SOUND that is in the names of all his prophets, and it is also Transliterated Yuh. What more proof can we asked for?

This is the most provable doctrine in the whole Bible. We can only hope to have this much conclusive evidence to prove all our other doctrines.

It is absolutely amazing how we have missed this all these years, when it is been right in front of us all the time.

What a coincidence it is, by leaving the YH alone, we get the exact same SOUND of Yuh that is in the prophets' names and the exact same SOUND of his name Yuh in Hallelujah, the name that went into all the earth, not to mention the exact same Yuh SOUND we get when the YH is Transliterated.

It appears that someone wants to have control over us and tell us to believe them instead of our own eyes and ears.

Psalm 68:4 says, "Sing unto "God", sing praises to his "name": "**extol**" him that rideth upon the heavens by his "name" JAH, and rejoice before him."

<u>Exo 15:2</u> Says, "The LORD *is* my strength and song, and he is become my salvation (Yeshua): he *is* my God, and I will prepare him an habitation; my father's God, and I will "**exalt**" him."

Side note: the capitals LORD in Exodus 15: 2 is actually "YH", NOT YHWH, and is this way 44 times as I know of, but notice the similarity between Exodus 15:2 and Psalm 68:4 concerning exalting his name YH.

It also appears that our God YH has become our salvation, and I believe this happened when he was made flesh, John 1:1-14 and 1st Timothy 3:16 etc. I'm getting a bit off tracked but you can find me on YouTube by typing in brother Arnold Bowen.

Which is it, is the SOUND of the name YH, pronounced Yuh, Yah or Yeh?

It can't be but one, and the transliteration of the YH is sounded Yuh, and that's the sound that the prophet

Moses heard, and he wrote it down. The MessYuh himself says that we are fools to be slow to believe ALL that the prophets have spoken Luke 24:25 KJV

[25] "Then he said unto them, "O fools", and slow of heart to believe "all" that the prophets have spoken: Moses is a prophet and he published the sacred name Yuh Wuh, according to the Transliteration of what Moses wrote that his name is.

Side note: Not only does the Hebrew have vowels sounds, these Semi vowels dates back to the 13th century BC According to Sass (5), already in the Middle Kingdom there were some cases of matres lectionis, i.e. consonant graphemes which were used to transcribe "vowels" in foreign words, namely in Punic (Jensen 290, Naveh 62), Aramaic, and "Hebrew" (ה, ו, י; sometimes even aleph א; Naveh 62). Naveh (ibid.) notes that the earliest Aramaic and "Hebrew" documents "already used matres lectionis". Some scholars argue that the Greeks must therefore have borrowed their alphabet from the Arameans. "However, the practice has older roots", as the Semitic cuneiform alphabet of Ugarit (13th century BC) already had matres lectionis

(Naveh 138)" see under Origins and Development at https://en.m.wikipedia.org/wiki/Mater_lectionis"

Chapter 5

Stolen Identity

The following facts eliminate any possibility for his name being pronounced Yahweh or Jehovah. **Neither of those names represent the self-existing God Almighty.**

Fact 1: In Hebrew, there's absolutely no "a" or "e" vowel between the YH, which are the vowels needed for the SOUND of the names Yah or Yeh, which kills any chance that his name might be Yahweh or Jehovah. I challenge anyone to show just one place where the A or E vowels are present between the YH, in the written Hebrew Scriptures, and I will hush. Ask yourself, where did these added uninspired vowels come from if they were not in their original Hebrew text?

Fact 2: Those names have to have an "a" or "e" vowel added between the YH, in order to make the Yah or

Yeh, SOUND, as in Yahweh or Jehovah, and there is none, they were added to the text, at a later date.

Fact 3: NOWHERE in the written word of God does an "a" or "e" vowel exist between the YH, which exposes the names Jehovah and Yahweh as not being the name of God. They show names to not represent the name of God.

Fact 4: The Hebrew Yod He makes the Yuh SOUND in Hebrew and when that SOUND is transliterated into other languages, SOUND for SOUND, it makes the SAME sound and is pronounced Yuh, in EVERY language, same as the Hebrew Yuh. This is true with the sound of the names of Hebrew cities like Bethlehem and Nazareth etc. Its said the same all over the world, and that is what transliteration of names is, and the name YHWH that Moses heard is no different, Moses published it.

Again, these FACTS absolutely eliminate the possibility of ANY other name than the original name YH, pronounced Yuh, and this is why we hear Hallelu Yuh in all the earth, NOT Hallelu Yeh or Yah.

I do not argue that the Masoretic vowels weren't added to the sacred name at a later date, which changed the SOUND/name, but that doesn't make it legitimate, "because to this day", there is "no A or E vowels that exist between the YH", they are added in an unlawful manner only, and the written Hebrew is still free form them today.

Chapter 6

Conclusive Evidence of the Name Yuh

The long form of his name is written in Hebrew approximately 7,000 times as יְהוּדָה and NOT once can we find an "a" or "e" vowel between the Hebrew Yod and He, which equals our English YH (Yuh) SOUND, and it's no coincidence that the Masoretic scribes NEVER added either of these two vowels into the sacred name YH, neither in the short form 49 times, nor the long form approximately 7,000 times, they respected the name too much to do such a thing.

יְהוּדָה

Hebrew is read from right to left, so notice that the Hebrew Yod He, (YH) is not touched by the Uninspired

Masoretic Vowel and therefore is not part of the sacred name, and never will be!!!

It's just not there, and people should stop wishing it in there, when they write or speak.

If these vowels, for the name Yahweh or Jehovah, is not between the YH in the written word of God, what more Proof do we need than that???

We don't need ANY more proof than the written word itself, but we can add a major proof to the written word, and that is the SOUND of his name, the YH (Yuh) which is written in the prophets' names, without the added vowels, and is ALWAYS pronounced Yuh, same as Hallelu Yuh!

Names like "Yuh" hoo daw
יְהוּדָה

Which means praise Yuh. Notice there's no vowel dots in the sacred name.

We see the two dots (:) "under" the Yod and He, but never in the name itself, because it is not a part of the original name, the vowel dots (:) were added to the name later.

Some suggest that the Masoretes added the vowels to the sacred name, but I find no evidence of this. They had approximately 7,049 times in scripture to add them, and NEVER did. The vowels were obviously added later.

Isa Yuh, which means Yuh has saved יְשַׁעְיָה

Notice this time God's name in Hebrew, the Yod He, is at the other end or far left, and STILL does not have an "a" vowel between the YH, proving it doesn't belong in the name of God. What's the matter with people?

Nehemiah, which means council of YH, pronounced Nehemi Yuh נְחֶמְיָה

Again, the Yod He is at the end of the name, and still no "a" vowel between the Yod and He, proving it is not in the original written word of God, which kills any possibility of the imposter name Yah, which is not the self-existing one.

I could go on all day with biblical names that has God's name in their names, like Nehemiah, Isaiah, Jeremiah, Elijah, Obadiah (עֹבַדְיָה)

and all biblical names ending in iah or jah is YH, with no added vowels between the YH, and is pronounced Yuh, which is the SOUND of the sacred name of God, just like in Hallelujah, which "jah" is also pronounced Yuh in every language and dialect in all the earth, and always makes the Yuh SOUND, because that is his name.

God's name, that is in all these prophets' names, never has the uninspired Masoretic vowels between the Yod and He, and to pollute their names with the uninspired vowels, it makes those names illegitimate also, because of the added vowels, and when we pull the uninspired A and E vowels back out from between the YH, the SOUND changes back and the names are legitimate again!

The original name YH is Pure, and unpolluted with these uninspired vowels, and makes the SOUND Yuh in all the earth!!! HalleluYuh

Think about this, there's absolutely no where in the "written" word of God, where the sacred name has an "a" or "e" vowel between the YH, neither in the shortened form YH, or the long form YHWH.

It can be conclusively proven that there is neither an "a" or "e" vowel between the original YH, simply by looking at the Hebrew YHWH, and the Masoretic vowel points, it makes the names Yahweh and Jehovah scripturally IMPOSSIBLE, and ending the debate!

If the "a" and "e" vowels do not exist anywhere in the written Hebrew, I ask you, who has the right or authority to add them, which drastically changes the word of God, by creating another name, and claiming that he is the self-existing one and giving praise to another name who did not create the heavens and earth, and is not the self-existing one?

Some things are hidden in simplicity. All we have to do is believe the SOUND of the name of God that we've actually been hearing every time we hear it in the names of his Prophets names, because the SOUND of "his name" is recorded in "their names", and is handed down to us, the same as the SOUND of his name in Hallelu Yuh is handed down to us.

Not once is there an "a" or "e" SOUND between the YH, of God's name or any of the prophets' names, and we ALWAYS get an involuntary U SOUND when pronouncing the YH of his name that is in the prophets' names or when pronouncing the original YH, without the added vowels. And if you don't believe me, get an unbiased child and place the YH before them, and they will pronounce it perfectly.

Matthew 21:16 says, "out of the mouth of babes he shall "perfect" praise".

A babe will tell the truth, just as our ancestors have told us the truth about the SOUND of his name in Hallelu Yuh, which means praise Yuh, NOT Yah or Yeh.

The same is true with the SOUND of God's name that's in his Prophets names, and is handed down to us today, same as Hallelu Yuh, is handed down, through **SOUND.**

We don't say Isa Yeh, Jeremi Yeh, Nehemi Yeh, or Hallelu Yeh or Yah. The SOUNDS of those names were never handed down to us from our ancestors, nor the SOUND of them ever been in the prophets' names, or ever memorialized!

Some people who don't want to accept all this conclusive evidence, start taking about things like people having different accents, as if that makes his name not be Yuh Wuh.

First of all, people have different accents, no matter what his name is, that does not change what their name is, why would it be any different with the name YHWH?

The SOUND of his name transcends or bypasses any accents. Anyone can hear the SOUND of a name, even a foreign name, and they can mimic or repeat the SOUND that they heard. Accents does not change his name from being what it is, this is just a smokescreen to try to get us away from the SOUND of his name that is in all the prophets' names.

Chapter 7

SOUND of the Name

Hearing is the most common way of communicating something to someone, and Faith comes by hearing the word of God.

The letters of any alphabet are not holy, but the SOUND that they cause us to make when pronouncing them is!

Again, once we hear what the **SOUND** of the name of God is, we then know his name and can share it with others by **SOUND**, because a name is a **SOUND**.

I am going to tell you what SOUND I heard my ancestors saying in church and you can tell me if you heard the same SOUND.

When saying hallelujah in church, I heard the SOUND Yuh, not Yah or Yeh. The SOUND Yuh was handed down to my family and my wife's family from our ancestors, through the word Hallelujah, pronounced Hallelu Yuh, and it is pronounced the same in every language and dialect all over the world today, just as he planned it to be, Romans 9:17 says,

"For the "scripture" saith unto Pharaoh, even for this same purpose have I raised thee up, that I might shew my power in thee, and that my name might be "declared" throughout all the earth."

Romans "9:16" is taken from Exodus "9:16", which says the same thing.

God's name is "still" in all the earth in the word Hallelujah, Pronounced Hallelu Yuh. Why is this so hard to see? We hear it with our own ears!

A name is a SOUND, and do we really believe that he raised Pharos up to declare his name in all the earth with a different SOUND other than Yuh, or do we think he declared a SOUND that needs an A or E between the original YH, which was later brought about by the uninspired Masoretic vowels?

Remember, we do not say Hallelu "Yeh", but Hallelu "Yuh", which is the same SOUND that his name makes in his prophets' names also!

He made the SOUND of his name known to us through the prophets' names and the word Hallelu Yuh, and the adversary is constantly attacking it.

We should no longer stand still for such an assault on the word of God, and the SOUND of his name.

The name of God is so important for salvation, healing, etc., and knowing his name has to do with him showing mercy on us.

Exodus 33:19 says,
[19] "And he said, I will make all my goodness pass before thee, and I will "proclaim" the name of the LORD before thee; and will be gracious to whom I will be gracious and will "shew mercy" on whom I will shew mercy."

He tells Moses that he is going to "proclaim" his name to him, and out of the same breath says I will have mercy on whom I will have mercy, showing that knowing how to pronounce his name has to do with mercy.

We know that YHWH "pronounced" his name to Moses and as a matter of fact one of the Hebrew definitions for "proclaim" is to "pronounce", i.e. his name, which had to do with showing mercy on Moses. There's no question that God correctly "pronounced" his name to Moses and Moses wrote it down, and the transliteration of what he wrote is Pronounced Yuh Wuh. He did not want his name miss pronounced throughout all the earth, and that is why everybody says hallelujah (Yuh) the same way in every language.

Complete Jewish Bible, actually says pronounce, it says, "He replied, "I will cause all my goodness to pass before you, and in your presence I will "pronounce" the name of Adonai. Moreover, I show favor to whomever I will, and I display mercy to whomever I will."

The Good News Translation says,
"The Lord answered, "I will make all my splendor pass before you and in your presence I will "pronounce" my sacred name. I am the Lord, and I show compassion and pity on those I choose."

Exodus 33:19–https://www.biblegateway.com/passage?search=Exodus%2033:19&version=GNT

Exodus 33:19–https://www.biblegateway.com/passage?search=Exodus%2033:19&version=CJB

What name has been proclaimed/pronounced the "same" throughout all the earth except Yuh, which is in Hallelu Yuh?

God had mercy on Moses by "pronouncing" his name to him, and once we know how to pronounce his name, then we can call upon it and he will answer us, and save us.

Joel 2:32 and Acts 2:21 says that in the last days God says that whoever calls on his name will be saved.

Paul says in Romans 10:13-14,
[13] "For whosoever shall call upon the name of the LORD (Yuh Wuh) shall be saved. [14] "How then shall they call on him in whom they have not believed?" and how shall they believe in him of whom they have not "heard"? and how shall they "hear" without a preacher?"

Acts 10:43 says

[43] "To him give all the prophets witness, that "through his name" whosoever believeth in him shall receive remission of sins."

You can read more about the **History of the Aramaic Language** at https://lifeenhancingideas.com/the-difference-between-aramaic-and-hebrew/ Which shows how Aramaic is a group of languages "or "dialects" of Semitic origin. It was spoken throughout the Assyrian and Babylonian Empires." And how the Messiah himself spoke Aramaic.

Peter's speech gave him away as being ""one of "them", referring to the Messiah's crew, because of his dialect. Adam Clark says on **Matthew 26:73**

"Thy speech—Thy manner of speech, η λαλια σου, that "dialect" of thine – "his accent being different" from that of Jerusalem."

Dialects don't change the name of God, but if it did, surely the Messiah knew how to pronounce the name and he spoke in the same Aramaic dialect as Peter, and that is why I say that the name of God is said the same in every language and dialect under heaven, same as Hallelu Yuh, and Yuh in the prophets' names, is said the same.

Just because they were speaking about the wonderful works of God, in different dialects, does not mean that each dialect had a different name for God. Remember, a name is a SOUND, and names are transliterated SOUND for SOUND and therefore the name of God is transliterated into every dialect and will make the same SOUND in each dialect or language.

We have the pure YH in scripture, with no vowels between it, which makes the Yuh SOUND as in Hallelu Yuh, and if we add an "a" between the YH, it makes a Yah SOUND, like in Yahweh, and if we add an E between the YH, it makes a Yeh SOUND as in Yehovah, but being left alone as written, it makes a Yuh SOUND as it does in the names of the prophets etc, and that is no coincidence.

No one on earth has the authority to add anything to the word of God, back then or now. And when we remove the added "a" and "e" vowels from the sacred name of God, the "SOUND" of his name goes back from the Yah and Yeh SOUND, to its original Yuh SOUND, as in Hallelu Yuh, and that is an absolute.

Many Christians don't realize that they are believing in and accepting the uninspired "a" or "e" vowels that were illegally added to the original word of God, as the word of God, or they would not partake in it themselves, every time they say Jehovah or Yahweh.

Nowhere in the Hebrew Scriptures can we find the Masoretic vowels ever added to the YH or YHWH, the addition of these unauthorized vowels was added at a later date, and even now, every time someone verbally says Jehovah or Yahweh, they are following the tradition of these men.

Now someone could prove me wrong, if they could produce one place where the written Hebrew has an "a" or "e" vowel added between the YH or the YHWH of his name, I will hold my tongue.

If it's not in there, why continue in the tradition of putting it in there?

Example, if the YH, which is pronounced Yuh, had an "e" vowel between the YH, which it doesn't, the name of God that is in the prophets' names would make the SOUND of Yeh, as in Yehovah, instead of Yuh, and everyone would be saying Hallelu "Yeh" in the churches, instead of Hallelu Yuh, and Isai Yeh, instead of Isai Yuh, and Eli Yeh instead of Eli Yuh, etc.

The bottom line is that the SOUND of the sacred name of God is in the Prophets names and is pronounced Yuh, and there is nothing no one can do to change the SOUND of the name of God that is in the prophet's names, which is Yuh, NOT Yah or Yeh!

It is already settled in heaven, and he will not change it for me or anyone else.

There's no way for anyone to get around this irrefutable evidence of the SOUND of the name of God in the prophet's names and that is how he protected the SOUND of his name and handed it down to us through the SOUND of his name which is in the prophets' names, and that way it can never be lost.

Many are searching to know how to pronounce the name of God, and it's so simple.

Once we hear the SOUND of God's name, by hearing it in the prophets' names and the word Hallelu Yuh, and the SOUND for SOUND transliteration, then we can turn around and pronounce it, it's that simple.

We hear the **SOUND** of God's name in the names of his prophets, like Nehemiah, Isaiah, Jeremiah, Elijah, and all biblical names ending in iah or jah are pronounced Yuh, which is the SOUND of the sacred name of God, just like in Hallelujah, which "iah" is also pronounced Yuh in every language in all the earth.

The reason all these prophets' names and many more biblical names that has the name of God in their names, all makes the same Yuh SOUND, is because that is the SOUND of the name of God, that he put in their names!

The "a" and "e" vowels don't belong in there and were NEVER a part of the sacred name, and by deductive reasoning, we know they were added later.

Nowhere in the written word of God, can we find one place where the Masoretes Jews put the "a" or "e" vowel into the YH, or the YHWH!

Therefore, you can place the YH or YHWH in front of a child, they will pronounce it "perfectly", because he says in Matthew 21:16 that he has perfected praise out of the mouth of babes. The babes were saying the forbidden name.

[16] "And said unto him, Hearest thou what these say? And Jesus saith unto them, Yea; have ye never read, Out of the mouth of babes and sucklings thou hast "perfected" praise?" A child will pronounce it perfectly.

Remember, once we hear the **SOUND** of the name of God, there's no reason we can't then turn around and pronounce it, and we hear the SOUND of his name in the prophets' names, and it is the Yuh SOUND, NOT the Yah or Yeh SOUND, so pronounce it. His name is Yuh Wuh.

We do not say Hallelu Yeh or Yah, but Hallelu Yuh, because the uninspired "e" and "a" was not part of the original name Yuh, but began to be added later, and we should not keep doing it, because no one has the authority to add to God's word, then or now.

Some struggle to make a case that the Masoretes put the vowel points into the name, to make the sacred name SOUND Yah or Yeh, instead of the original Yuh SOUND, if so, then why didn't it work, we still say IsaYuh, etc?

His name that is in the prophet's names still make the same Yuh SOUND, not Yeh. It doesn't say Nehemi Yeh, but Nehemi Yuh, nor Jeremi Yeh, instead of Jeremi Yuh, and Hallelu Yeh, instead of Hallelu Yuh, therefore if the Masoretes put the vowels to make everyone say Yah or Yeh, it did not work, because we still say IsaYuh etc. The vowels were added AROUND the sacred name to remind the reader not to read the name, but say Adonai or Elohim instead.

We have scholars with the name YH (Yuh) in their names like Jerem(iah), Nehem(iah), etc, who believes the pronunciation SOUND of God's name is (Jeh) ovah, yet they still keep the SOUND of God's name (Yuh) that is in their name, they don't claim the name Nehemi Yuh to be pronounced Nehemi Gee or Yeh, as in Jehovah, they leave the YH/Yuh SOUND in their name alone, but change the SOUND of the YH in God's name to Jeh or some other SOUND, and protect the Yuh SOUND in their own names.

If they are going to change the SOUND of the YH in his name, to YEH or Yah, why don't they also change the Yuh SOUND in their own names to a Yeh or Yah SOUND, like they do his, and then say Hallelu Yeh? You cannot have it both ways.

And why don't little children and everyone pronounce the YH, as Yeh, instead of Yuh when the Transliterated name is placed before them?

I believe anyone who continues to pollute his holy name, in the same way they did, by adding uninspired Vowels, are just as guilty as the ones that started it in the first place!

He that makes a lie will have their part in the lake of fire, according to Revelation 21:8.

The very introduction to this article proves what the "SOUND" of the name of God is, without reading anything else.

When the wise and prudent scholar get through arguing whether it's the "a" or "e" vowel that should be placed between the original YH, (which is neither) they admit that they really don't know for sure, because no one was alive back then.

Who says that any Masoretic vowels needs to be placed between the original YH in the first place?

When using the SOUND approach, you would not have had to live back then, to know the SOUND of his name, all we need to know is the SOUND of his name now, today.

We do not have to try to wade through all the confusion of the wise and prudent scholars, and all the speculation, conjecture, assumptions, and the guessing as to which of the uninspired vowels they should place between the inspired YH, to obtain the pronunciation of the name of God, when we have the SOUND that his name makes, right before our own big ears, and after all their guessing is over, it is still their best guess, and I want no part of it, especially when we have the SOUND of his name recorded in the Prophets names and the word Hallelujah (Yuh) to go by, not to mention the Transliteration of the name itself.

To say no one knows his name shows how biblically illiterate they are, because the Bible teaches that his people will know his name, and everyone who calls on it in the last days will be saved. How can we call on his name if we don't know it?

He put the SOUND of His name in the Prophets' names, and whatever SOUND his name makes in their names, that is the same SOUND that Moses heard and is handed down to us today, by knowing the prophets names, and nothing has changed, the SOUND that the name of God makes in all the prophets names is Yuh, as in Hallelu Yuh, Isai Yuh, Jeremi Yuh, Eli Yuh, Yuh hoo daw, Nehemi Yuh, etc, it's the SOUND of his name that we are listening for, and all the confusion in the world can NOT change that. We are looking for the SOUND of his name, not Masoretes vowels to add to the word of God.

Example, the tribe of Judah is a very large tribe of people, and there's no way for all of them to forget the "SOUND" of the head of their tribes name, which is Yuh hoo daw in Hebrew, and means praise YH (Yuh), and the YH is ALWAYS pronounced Yuh, and if you don't believe it, place the YH before any unbiased child or English professor, and they will say Yuh every time. Transliteration is the reason Hallelujah, pronounced Hallelu Yuh is said the same way all over the world.

Here is the Hebrew for the name Judah, which is actually pronounced Yuh hoo daw, without the added E vowel.

"H3063
יְהוּדָה
yehûdâh
yeh-hoo-daw'

From H3034; celebrated; Jehudah (or Judah), the name of five Israelites; also of the tribe descended from the first, and of its territory:–Judah."

Unlike English, Hebrew reads from right to left, and you can see for yourself the inspired name YH written in Hebrew letters, with the created Masoretic vowels dangling around it, just waiting for someone to later add them to the inspired scriptures, which they eventually did, but with God's Infinite wisdom, they cannot get away with it because of the Yuh SOUND that the YH makes, and always made in the many biblical names, which has his name in them, so that the SOUND of his name can never be lost or forgotten. יְהוּדָה **His name will endure as long as the sun.** Psalm 72:17.

Noticed that the Hebrew Yod He, is not touched by the Uninspired Vowel and therefore is not part of the sacred name!

Even though God's name is known in many prophets' name, it says,
[1] "In Judah (Yuh hoo daw) is "God known": "his name" is great in Israel." Psalm 76:1.

When we listen to the SOUND that the YH made when God preserved or recorded it in many Hebrew names like Yuh hoo daw (which means worship or praise Yuh. (Judah), and also many of the prophets with the same

YH in their names, carries the exact same SOUND that the YH makes today, and that SOUND is Yuh.

When the YH is placed before an unbiased child or anyone, for pronouncing, they will say Yuh, the same Yuh SOUND that was handed down to all the earth in the word Hallelujah, which is pronounced Hallelu Yuh, all making the same SOUND of the YH, as being Yuh in EVERY case, which conclusively proves God's name is SOUNDED Yuh, NOT Yah or Yeh! There's no other option.

Having this clear "SOUND" evidence, it is undeniable that his name makes no other SOUND other than Yuh, as it did then, and as it does today, what else can it be?

Why deny the obvious and add an uninspired "A" or "E" vowel which changes the SOUND from the original Yuh SOUND, to Yah or Yeh SOUND, which is not the SOUND of the self-existing one?

The Yah or Yeh SOUND was never handed down to us from our ancestors, we don't say Hallelu Yeh or Hallelu Yah, but Hallelu Yuh.

Remember that a name is a SOUND, and when we deny the SOUND, we deny his name, and Revelation speaks of those that have not denied his name shall enter.

Nowhere in the written Hebrew text is the Masoretic vowels ever connected to the sacred name! They were put there to remind the reader not to say the name, not to later be added to it.

There's absolutely no evidence that the Masoretes intended that the vowels were ever to become a part of the sacred name, or they would have put it into the Tetragrammaton themselves. As a matter of fact, the evidence shows that they NEVER touched the name with these vowels. All one has to do is look at the YH and the YHWH in the Hebrew, and you can see that this is true, by deductive reasoning making it so obvious that someone added an uninspired "a" or "e" to the name, at a later date, which changed the SOUND of the original name, making it void, and giving God's glory to another name.

It's Jeremi Yuh, NOT Jeremi Yeh. Its Eli Yuh, NOT Eli Yeh, its Nehemi Yuh, NOT Nehemi Yeh, etc.

Therefore, the uninspired vowels were added to the name by someone at a later date, and we should NOT follow them or their tradition. The truth will make us free.

Psalm 91:14 -15 says,
"Because he hath set his love upon me, therefore will I deliver him: I will set him on high, "because he hath "known" my name." 15 He shall call upon me, and I will answer him: I *will be* with him in trouble; I will deliver him and honour him."

How would you like to claim those promises because you know his name?

The most common or ordinary way of communicating something is by "hearing". They did not have printing presses and faith comes by hearing.

Romans 10:13 and 17-18 says, Romans 10:13 Says, [13] "For whosoever shall call upon the name of "the Lord" (Yuh wuh) shall be saved."...

[17] "So then faith cometh by "hearing", and "hearing" by the word of God. [18] But I say, have they not

"heard"? Yes verily, their "SOUND" went into all the earth, and their words unto the ends of the world."

Perhaps this will help you understand.

What if the short form of his name was Tom instead of Yuh, and the long-form Tommy, and we read about how the Almighty Tom done this and that and also the Prophets names had the name Tom in their names, would you say that the name of God was Tom?

What if Psalm 68:4 said, "Sing unto God, sing praises to "his name": extol him that rideth upon the heavens by his "name Tom, and rejoice before him."

We would have no scriptural choice but the say his name is Tom, the short form of Tommy.

What if it said Eli Tom, which would mean my God is Tom, instead of Eli Yuh which means my God is Yuh, we would say the name of God is Tom.

What if it said "Tom" hoo daw, which would mean praise Tom, instead of Yuh hoo daw, which means praise Yuh.

It's the SOUND that tells us his name because a name is a SOUND, and it is not lost!

Psalm 72:17 says,
"His name shall endure for ever: his "name shall be continued as long as the sun": and *men* shall be blessed in him: all nations shall call him blessed."

Psalm 135:17 says,
"Thy name, O LORD, *endureth* for ever; *and* thy memorial, O LORD, throughout all generations."

The transliteration of the sacred name tells us how to pronounce it, and also reveals what that SOUND is, in all languages and dialects on earth.

When Judah's mother named him in Genesis 29:35, there were no Masoretic vowel points to deal with, nor in the Dead Sea Scrolls etc.

Again, He put the SOUND of His name in the Prophets names, and whatever SOUND his name made in their names, that same SOUND is his name, and is handed down to us today, by knowing their names.

By knowing the "SOUND" of his name, that is in their names, we conclusively know the SOUND of his name, and nothing can change that.

Again, the tribe of Judah is a large tribe of people, and there's no way for all of them to forget the "SOUND" of the name of the head of their tribe, which is YH (Yuh) hoo daw in Hebrew, and means praise YH, and the YH is ALWAYS pronounced Yuh, NOT Yah or Yeh.

Here is the Hebrew for the name Judah.

H3063
יְהוּדָה
yehûdâh
yeh-hoo-daw'

From H3034; celebrated; Jehudah (or Judah), the name of five Israelites; also, of the tribe descended from the first, and of its territory:–Judah."

Unlike English, Hebrew reads from right to left, and you can see for yourself the inspired name YH in Hebrew letters, with the created vowel hanging around it, just waiting for someone to add them to the inspired scriptures, which they eventually did, but with God's Infinite wisdom, they cannot get away with it because of the Yuh SOUND that the YH makes and has always made in the many biblical names. יְהוּדָה

Noticed that in Hebrew, the Yod He, is never touched by the Uninspired Vowel and therefore it is not part of the sacred name. The uninspired "a" and "e" vowels were later shoved between the Y and H and the YHWH, which changed the original SOUND from Yuh, to Yah or Yeh, which is breaking the third commandment by falsifying it!

In other words, the "a" or "e" vowels are hanging underneath or around the sacred name, but it's not a part of the name, that came along later, when someone came along, not understanding the vowels were there to remind the readers not to read the sacred name, but instead, say Adonai or something else.

Nowhere in the "written word" of God does the YH or YHWH have one of these uninspired vowels between them, and this is something you can verify for yourself by looking at the Hebrew.

What conclusive evidence is there for the SOUND of the YH or YHWH ever making a Yeh or Yah SOUND???

The bottom line is the A and the E vowels are solely based upon the Masoretic vowels that someone later added into the sacred text, changing the SOUND of the sacred name.

When these, created, Masoretic vowels were later added to the Tetragrammaton, we now have a new SOUND, namely the Yah and Yeh SOUND, versus the original SOUND of Yuh, that the YH makes without them, and is still SOUNDED Yuh in Hallelu Yuh and the prophets' names, all over the world.

The Hebrew letters Yod He Waw He, when Transliterated into other languages like English etc, and in English, the Hebrew Yod He Waw He is equivalent to the SOUND of our English YHWH. Now all we have to do is get an unbiased child or anyone for that matter, to SOUND, or pronounce it, and we will have the same SOUND of the name that Moses heard, Exodus 3:15, and which he captured with his alphabet Yod He Waw He, which equals our YHWH SOUND!

True Sound of the Sacred Name of God

I am pointing you back to the original SOUND that the name of God made, before someone added the uninspired "a" or "e" vowel to it.

Exodus 15:2 uses the short form of the name of God in everyday conversation, and it has LORD in all capitals where the YH is.

"The LORD (YH) *is* my strength and song, and he is become my salvation: he *is* "my God", and I will prepare him an habitation; my father's God, and I will "exalt" him."

H3050

יָהּ

yâhh

yaw

Contracted for H3068, and meaning the same; *Jah*, the sacred name:–Jah, the Lord, most vehement. Cp. names in "-iah," "-jah."

Total KJV occurrences: 49

We have inherited lies, and we need to be different, a peculiar people, and use his true name that we've heard all our lives with our own ears, or should we just go along with the lies that we are told?

Jeremiah 16:19-21 says, "O LORD, my strength, and my fortress, and my refuge in the day of affliction, the Gentiles shall come unto thee from the ends of the earth, and shall say, Surely our fathers have "inherited lies", vanity, and *things* wherein *there is* no profit. Shall a man make gods unto himself, and they *are* no gods?

Therefore, behold, I will this once cause them to know, I will cause them to know mine hand and my might; and they shall know that "my name" *is* The "LORD."

We would think the word Hallelujah would change a little bit in some of the many languages throughout the whole earth, but it appears to have started off as hallelujah and is still hallelujah today the same SOUND in all the earth, this is a miracle in itself.

When God said he raised pharaoh up so that his name would be declared throughout all the earth, what's the odds of someone picking a Yuh SOUND that is said the same in all the earth, and that same Yuh SOUND just happen to be in all the Prophets names, and the same Yuh SOUND just happens to mean God this or God that, and the same Yuh SOUND just happens to match the SOUND of the Hebrew transliteration of the Hebrew Yod He Waw He (Tetragrammaton).

And how could the Yuh SOUND not be the SOUND of the name of God?

How can a totally different SOUND, created by using uninspired vowels and adding them into the scriptures be his name instead of the name Yuh?

They were saying hallelujah in China and in Russia, Europe, and all over the world they were saying the same SOUND hallelujah and it hasn't changed yet and will not change in none of these countries. How is that possible?

Hallelujah is not a resent SOUND it goes on back past horse and buggy days, it goes back past cowboy days, back to leaving Egypt.

When we deny the SOUND of his name, the name that we've been hearing all our lives since birth, is to deny the SOUND that the Transliterated Hebrew letters Yod He Waw He makes, which SOUND is equivalent to the SOUND of our English letters YHWH, which produces the SOUND of Yuh Wuh, when pronounced by an unbiased person, and this is an undeniable fact, and the SOUND that the Yod He Waw He makes, is the name of our God, which also is an undeniable FACTS!

It is the SOUND that went into all the earth with the word Hallelu, which means praise and Yuh is his Holly name. Hallelu Yuh.

To deny his name is also to deny the SOUND of his name, Yuh, that he put in the names of all his prophets, which we've been hearing and saying, especially the Hebrew speaking people.

How can we deny the SOUND of his name, Yuh, that we've been hearing and saying all our lives, which SOUND is handed down to us from our ancestors? How can we deny it when we've already heard it? To deny it is to deny life itself.

Yet some will deny it because of the so-called wise and prudent scholars, but this old country boy is going to stick with what his ears are actually hearing, and not with what some scholars are saying.

When I hear the sound of the Father's name Yuh, which is in the names of his Prophets, and in Hallelu Yuh, I clearly hear a distinct Yuh sound.

Should we deny the sound of his name Yuh, the SOUND that the YH makes, the SOUND that we are hearing, and go with the sound of one of the names that some scholars are saying?

I can't help but hearing the sound of his name that the YH makes, as being Yuh, not Yah or Yeh, and I can't deny it.

Hallelujah

Give me that old time religion

Chapter 8

The Vaw or the Wah SOUND.

As of now, the author believes the V SOUND is influenced by the German language.

Even among the Hebrew speaking people, there is a big debate going on over the original SOUND of the V and W. Why is this?

Before the Hebrew people were scattered to Germany etc, there was no problem, they were all on the same page concerning the pronunciation of the name.

If the original SOUND was a V SOUND, there would be no debate, because the ones who didn't go to Germany would still have the V SOUND same as the ones who did. But if the original SOUND was a W

SOUND, I can see how those that went to Germany would eventually adapt to the German language, which has a V SOUND instead of the W SOUND and then the problem begins.

Again, if it was originally a V SOUND, then the ones who didn't scatter to Germany would still have the V SOUND, just like the ones who did, and then there's nothing to debate, because everyone is still on the V SOUND.

The goal of the Mesorites was to add vowels around the sacred name to make everyone say Adonai instead of the true sacred name Yuh Wuh and then someone come along and put the vowels into the name itself to make them say Yahweh or Jehovah instead of the true sacred name Yuh Wuh. It appears that both methods are working today.

The second group of people following the tradition not to say the sacred name, which possibly could have been more zealous men of the Masoretes, or another group, took a different approach by adding vowels between the YH, having people say Yahweh or Jehovah instead of the true name YHWH, pronounced

Yuh Wuh, protecting anyone from blaspheming, and it worked and is still working today, and that in itself is amazing when it is so obvious that the SOUND of sacred name is Yuh Wuh, and everyone knows there's no vowels in Hebrew between the YH, except most Gentiles. Now we have the orthodox Jews saying Adonai instead of the name Yuh Wuh, and all the other nations (Gentiles) saying Yahweh or Jehovah, instead of the true name Yuh Wuh.

It appears that these Jews, knowing that they could not get the Gentiles to follow Jewish tradition and say Adonai, so with these uninspired vowels, they created the names Yahweh and Jehovah for them to say instead of the sacred name Yuh Wuh.

The second group used a different approach to accomplish the same thing. The added vowels to the name YH (Yuh) changed the SOUND of it to a totally different name, namely Jehovah or Yahweh, thus they were protecting the True SOUND of the name Yuh Wuh, from the Gentiles who did not know enough about the Hebrew language, to know that there are no vowels between the YH, for the names Jehovah and Yahweh, and it is still working today.

Remember, they were protecting the true SOUND of the name of God, by having the Jews saying Adonai, and the Gentiles saying Yahweh or Jehovah.

The bogus names Yahweh and Jehovah are just another way to keep people from saying the true sacred name YHWH as written by Moses.

As long as they keep people saying Adonai, Yahweh, or Jehovah, they are keeping them from saying the sacred name Yuh Wuh, which is their goal. People today are not servants of Yuh Wuh, but unwittingly servants of the Jews, and do not even know it.

The Yahweh people came out of using the name Jesus, when they found out it was erroneous and that there was no letter J, for the name Jesus.

Let's pray they do the same with the names Jehovah and Yahweh, when they find out that there's no letter A or E between the YH in the written Hebrew language, making these names illegitimate, because of the created Masoretes vowels being added between the YH.

Chapter 9

What are our options concerning the SOUND of the sacred name of God?

The SOUND of his name is real evidence and is the best witness as to what his name is, not what other people say it is, by using a lot of speculating, guessing, conjecture, hearsay, assumptions, etc, but using SOUND, which is fact!

We have three major SOUND we are looking at, concerning the YH, Yuh, Yah, and Yeh. What could cause someone to skip over the original YH/Yuh SOUND as in Hallelu Yuh, the name of God, that went into all the earth, and pick the Yeh or Yah SOUND that some man may or may not have said or written, that his name might be???

James Adair, who lived among the American Indians for many years and wrote a book on them, how he believes they are Israelites and says they say his name is YOHEWAH and makes a compelling case that the American Indians are descendants of the Israelites, but even if he is right, that does not conclusively prove that they are SOUNDING his name right and that he is hearing it right. Nothing conclusive.

The SOUND I hear them chanting is Yuh Yuh Yuh Wuh Yuh Yuh Yuh Wuh, my point is who are we to believe, nearly all these reports SOUND believable?

I believe he wanted his name pronounced correctly throughout all the earth and he pronounced it correctly to Moses, and Moses wrote it down, and the transliteration of the name that he wrote down is Yuh Wuh, which anyone can easily verified in a few minutes, if there are people around to ask to sound the YHWH for you.

Using the sound of our English YHWH letters, it can not make any other sound other than Yuh Wuh, when sounding these letters!

The same is true with the sound of the Hebrew letters Yod He Waw He, it can only make the Yuh Wuh sound.

There are many options to choose from, because people come up with many different SOUNDS for the name of God, and they all have their reasons for their beliefs, but they all can't be right and could all be wrong.

Most of them study and go into ancient manuscripts etc and try to see what the SOUND of God's name is, but they cannot even agree among themselves, therefore, after we study each one of their arguments, should we just pick the one that makes the best argument?

Some argue that Greek writings reveals the sacred name, like IABE was pronounced Yahweh, but we do not know for sure these letters are even right, must less how they were being pronounced and can we really trust it, especially when people have been hiding the name?

In our English Bibles His name is written iah at the end of many biblical names, but is pronounced Yuh, as in hallelujah, Isaiah, Jeremiah, Nehemiah, Obadiah, etc, not Yah!

Psalm 68:4 says his name is Yah, which is the same as the iah, and it should be pronounced Yuh also.

Psalms 68:4
(**KJV**) "Sing unto "God", sing praises to his "name": extol him that rideth upon the heavens by "his name "JAH", and rejoice before him."

People argue that his name is this or that, after he repeatedly tells us his name through the SOUND of his name that is in the names of his Prophets, and that SOUND of his name is Yuh that went into all the earth.

How would you feel if someone insisted on calling you something different than what you keep telling them what your name is?

That is very disrespectful, especially when he tells us so many times, what his name is, in the prophets' names and Hallelu Yuh, not to mention the transliteration of the Tetragrammaton, which is Yuh Wuh.

Deuteronomy 32:3 KJV says,
[3] "Because I will "publish the name" of the "LORD": ascribe ye greatness unto our God."

We must believe the prophet Moses or be fools.

Luke 24:25 KJV says,
[25] "Then he said unto them, "O fools", and slow of heart to believe "all" that the prophets have spoken:"

The Messiah calls them fools for being slow to believe all that the prophets have spoken, which would include the prophet Moses.

Luke 16:31 KJV says,
[31] "And he said unto him, If they "hear not Moses" and the prophets, neither will they be persuaded, though one rose from the dead."

The Messiah teaches that we are to believe the writings of Moses

John 5:47 says,
[47] "But if ye believe not his **"writings"**, how shall ye believe my words?"

My point is that God told the prophet Moses what the SOUND of his name is, and the prophet Moses wrote it down, so he could publish it, and because of tradition of men, people have a problem believing what Moses wrote down.

I believe the 4 Hebrew letters, Yod He Waw He, that he wrote down, which is equals to the SOUND of our YHWH, when transliterated, and is pronounced Yuh Wuh, as in Hallelu Yuh is the correct SOUND of his name, because it is the same sound of his name that is in the names of his prophets!

We must believe the writings of Moses, and he didn't write a name that the sound can't be specifically published, and leave the door open for everyone to add what vowels they want to add to the name he already wrote, to make the name sound what they think it should sound.

I do not believe the Greek A, in IABE, must make a hard A SOUND for the name Yah! As a matter of fact, his name Yuh, that is in ALL the many biblical names ending in "iah" or "jah" makes the Yuh SOUND, with a soft U, as in Hallelujah (Hallelu Yuh), the SOUND of his name that went into all the earth, **not a hard A SOUND**.

The SOUND we hear in ALL biblical names with the name of God in their names, like Isaiah, Jeremiah, Obadiah, Elijah, Nehemiah, and many more cannot all be wrong.

None of the many many SOUNDS of names that they come up with are in harmony with the SOUND of his name Yuh that went into all the earth, and is said the same in every language, yet they choose the SOUND of one of those many names above the SOUND of his true name that went into all the earth, and that SOUND is Yuh.

We can reject and deny that SOUND if we like, but a name is a SOUND and when we deny and reject the SOUND, we deny and reject his name.

The A between the YH in the prophets' names still makes the Yuh SOUND and if we pull it out, it **still** makes the Yuh SOUND in all the names ending in iah and jah, because his name is Yuh. A name is not just some written letters, but a SOUND.

We must find out the SOUND of his name before we can know what his name is.

Here are some well-known facts.

1. We know the **SOUND** of the Transliterated Yod He is equivalent to our YH and is pronounced Yuh, as in Hallelu Yuh.

2. We know the SOUND of the YH in all the prophets' names is also pronounced Yuh.

3. We know the SOUND of his name that went into all the earth is also pronounced Yuh, because that is his name, and when he pronounced his name to Moses, it would not be any different.

4. We know that in light of the conclusive evidence above, his name is Yuh.

Fact #

5. We "do not know" if what people have been telling us is 100% true. I could list a bunch of stuff that we don't know, but I won't right now.

There will be many **religious** people that will come to him in that day asking if they were using the right name saying, Lord Lord did we not do this and that in your name? And he will say to them depart from me you that work in equity, I never knew you, Matthew 7:22.

Some of the many RELIGIOUS people, in Matthew 7:22 could be Yahweh and Jehovah people along with the Jesus people etc and everyone who rejects the sacred SOUND of his name Yuh Wuh.

We don't want our loved ones or ourselves to be in that number.

Let's put the shoe on the other foot for a minute.

What if the sound of his name, that is in all the prophets names, was a Yeh or Yah sound, as Eli Yeh or Yah, Isa Yeh or Yah, Jeremi Yeh or Yah, Nehemi Yeh or Yah, and Hallelu Yeh or Yah, etc, wouldn't we then say that that is the sound of his name, or would we then say the sound is Yuh, even if Yuh was not the sound we hear in the prophets names?

And on top of that, what if the Transliteration of the sound of the YH, was Yeh or Yah, would we insist on calling him Yuh, even if Yuh was not the sound of the transliteration?

Certainly not, we would correctly say that the sound of his name is Yeh or Yah, because that's the sound we hear, not Yuh, a sound that we did not hear. Why can't we do the same with the Yuh sound that we hear, because that's the sound of the name that we are hearing?

Is it because of tradition or something that we have been told by people that we think are smarter than us, that we can't accept what we are hearing with our own ears?

As I said, this book conclusively proves what the "SOUND" of the name of God is.

We have proven that when we've found the SOUND of his name, we've actually found his name, because a name is a SOUND, and then we can share the SOUND/NAME with others.

By taking this approach to finding the true name of God, the "SOUND" approach, which is different from the wise and prudent scholars' approach, who tried to find his name by using the uninspired vowels from the Masoretic text, we can conclusively prove what his name is, and everyone who calls on it will be saved, Joel 2:32.

The new approach is to find the true SOUND of the sacred name, and when we do, we've found the true name of God, because a name is a SOUND.

I've never heard God's name make any other SOUND than the SOUND Yuh, as it is SOUNDED in the names of his prophets, and in the name Hallelu Yuh, and the Yuh sound that the YH makes when transliterated into English.

This book has conclusively shown what the SOUND of God's name is. As I said, some things are hidden in simplicity.

Again, we hear with our own ears, the distinct SOUND of his name "Yuh", that is in the prophets' names, and we now see with our own eyes that there's no A or E vowel between the YH in the written Hebrew language, which A or E vowel is absolutely necessary for the name of Jehovah and Yahweh, and if its not there, it makes the names Jehovah and Yahweh scripturally IMPOSSIBLE, which I have shown.

We simply believe, like a little child, and a little child has no problem pronouncing the YHWH as Yuh Wuh, which is the correct Transliteration of the Hebrew Yod He Waw He, and we must humble ourselves and become as a little child to be saved, Matthew 18:3.

Hope that this book has got you to thinking that if we don't add an A or E vowel between the YH, the YH will then make a Yuh SOUND, as in Hallelu Yuh, which is the name of God that went into all the earth, in the word Hallelu Yuh, and is pronounced the same in every language.

And also makes the Yuh SOUND of the name of God that is in the prophets' names, names like Isa Yuh, Jeremi Yuh, Eli Yuh, Yuh hoo daw, etc. and that this is no coincidence, because YH (Yuh) is his name, and is obviously SOUNDED Yuh, not Yah or Yeh.

The last option is, we can ignore all of this conclusive evidence and take it up with him on judgment day and explain to him why we chose to continue using the sound of other names like YahWeh and Jehovah, when there's no A or E vowel between the YH in the original Hebrew text, for the SOUND of either of these names.

"Truth is freedom", he said you shall know the truth and the truth will make you free, and we are now free from calling on names that does not represent the name of our God.

We are free and no longer give glory, honor, and praise to a totally different name, with a totally different SOUND, other than the SOUND of the name of our God and Saviour, Yuh Wuh. Hallelu Yuh.

Due to the extreme urgency of getting this book out, I am publishing it with the intent to have my pastor brother Matthew Janzen edit it, and add more specific information, which will conclusively prove what has already been conclusively proven in this book, if that is possible.

I wanted to talk a little more about The Ugarit Text, which Brother Matthew can do in the next book. The Ugarit Text is among the oldest writings ever found, and in them, it says the son of God's name is Y–W, which is pronounced Yuh Wuh, same as YH-WH, which is pronounced Yuh-Wuh etc.

In the Ugarit Text, the YW is written with only 2 letters, YW, but makes the same identical SOUND as the Hebrew YH-WH, that is found in the Hebrew text.

Abraham owned all the land of Canaan, Gen 17:8, and the name of Abraham's God is YHWH, which they pronounced with only 2 letters, YW.

His name is written YW, YHW, YHWH, and YH, psalm 68:4, all are pronounced, Yuh, or Yuh-wuh.

The Ugaritic text is "KTU 1.1 IV 14: which says, sm . bny . **yw** . ilt

My point in bringing up this ancient historical evidence, showing that the SOUND of the name of God was present in the land that God gave to Abraham and was pronounced Yuh Wuh. Anyone interested can see the chapter that Brother Matthew Janzen will add, along with much more information, in the next addition.

Does knowing his name really matter?

Laying aside all the many scriptures that says if we call on his name we will be saved etc., I find the following two scriptures interesting.

Psalm 79:6 says,
[6] "Pour out thy wrath upon the heathen that have not known thee, and upon the "kingdoms" that have not called upon thy name."

Jeremiah 10:25 says,
[25] "Pour out thy fury upon the heathen that know thee not, and upon the "families that call not on thy name": for they have eaten up Jacob, and devoured him, and consumed him, and have made his habitation desolate."

Remember, TRUTH is FREEDOM, and once we know it, our lives will never be the same, we will be new creatures in the Messiah/MessYuh, Anointed Yuh. Hallelu Yuh.

Go to Youtube and type in Brother Arnold Bowen for videos

Brother Arnold Bowen at 3466 E. high tower Trail Conyers, GA 30012

Website http://lunarsabbath.info

Email lunarsabbath@aol.com and list other books

Radio station WWCR Live broadcast at http://wwcr.gsradio.net:3863/index.html?sid=1 Saturday 7:30 Pm Est and 4:00 Pm Thursday, click on listen

Also TUESDAY at 7:00 PM Est click on

http://wwcr.gsradio.net:3763/index.html?sid=1 And click on listen

Also Monday through Thursday at 10:15 Est 3.215, and Saturday at 10:15, on 3.215

Reference books used is the KJV Bible

Adam Clark Commentary
Strong's Concordance
The Interlinear Bible Hebrews and Greek by Jay P. Green Sr.

Printed in the USA
CPSIA information can be obtained
at www.ICGtesting.com
LVHW011540040224
770897LV00002B/422